Become the Employer of Choice

Table of contents

Preface

As we were writing this book in 2019, almost all employers were scratching their heads trying to figure out how to hire more employees. We firmly believe that the 2018-2019 era will be remembered as the sales restricted period due to not being able to hire enough employees.

As we finish up this book here in 2020, we are currently in the middle of a pandemic crisis due to the Covid-19 virus. The current situation is jumping unemployment and a very uncertain future.

While most businesses are in full-on panic, the need for a high-performing team is still a constant. It may even be more important – post crisis. The good news is finding new team members will most likely be easier going forward. However, having the "right people on the bus," as Jim Collins once said, is still ultra-critical.

So, when it comes to building that high-performing team…

What if we could show you a better way?

Would you listen?

Are you ready?

- What if we could help you build a high(er) performing team? (You probably think your team is already a high-performing team).
- What if we could help you raise the engagement level of your current team?
- What if we could help you become the employer of choice in your industry, or in your geographic area?

We know, this all sounds idealistic and absolutely not possible. You are now thinking we are absolute kooks. But we assure you, we have clients that have achieved the above items. All the above items. Real life. Real results.

So now, somewhat in disbelief, you are going to ask for the cliff notes version or the silver bullets to achieve all of this…. this week. Slow down, Sparky, it will not happen that easily or quickly. But it will happen if you follow the steps.

A long time ago we worked in large corporations that were employee magnets- and it was not because they were great places to work. However, they did have systems that made attracting great employees and building a great team, work.

In today's world the large corporations do not have the edge. You do. Why? Because you have more flexibility, autonomy, and can act quicker. Plus, you have the huge advantage of being personable and more family oriented. This is what today's workers crave.

That said, this book is specifically written for the privately-owned business leader. While you may fear large corporations…. please don't!

While the large corporations have more systems, more resources, and a more recognizable name, the privately-owned businesses will always be more agile, more employee-friendly, more dynamic, and more endearing to the individual employee.

Through working with many businesses as business/executive coaches, we can substantiate the fact that most businesses, especially privately-owned businesses, do not really focus on building a high-performance culture and/or a high-performance team. Most are more focused on the day-to-day "grind." We further believe that the reason that this is lacking is because of one or more of the following:

- They simply do not know how to do it.

  In this book, we will show you very easy, effective tips to building your high-performance team for your business.

- They do not believe in the positive benefits of a high-performance team.

  In over 14 years of helping clients become dominant in their industry or geographic area, we can give countless great examples of businesses that have achieved this level of performance. Been there, done that! This book is a summary of very effective methods based on real experience, not theory.

- They are simply procrastinating and will do it "later."

  Many business owners/leaders simply put this off, planning to do it "later." Building a high-performance team is something that needs to be done in small steps, daily. This is not a "2-week project" that we can do later. It is a straightforward process. If you have not started this earlier, start it now!

Come along with us as we go through a quick journey on very simple steps to build your successful high-performance team. Don't put it off anymore. Your competitors may already be working on this and may surpass you, leaving you in the dust.

If after reading this book you are still not convinced, visit our website, or call us:

Rick Munson

Business/Executive Coach

Paramount Business Development, Inc.

www.paramountbusinessdevelopment.com

745 Main Street

Suite 205

Stroudsburg, Pa 18360

1-570-517-7100

Bill Skinner

Business/Executive Coach

Paramount Business Development, Inc.

www.paramountbusinessdevelopment.com

745 Main Street

Suite 205

Stroudsburg, Pa 18360

1-570-517-7100

Acknowledgements

This may be hard to understand as you are reading this, but we hate to write! We do everything possible to not have to write. We are slow at it, lousy at it…oh, and did we mention we hate it!? We would highly prefer working with a client to help them improve their leadership, and/or their company.

So, as you are reading this, we must thank those that really made this possible.

<u>Jenny Kane</u>. The most amazing administrative/marketing assistant. Through her thorough and quiet ways, she kept encouraging us to write. She has been extremely supportive in this effort, and most importantly in our business in general. She was also instrumental in publishing our prior three books:

> "Sales Magic: 12 Steps to Achieve Massive Sales Growth"

> "Fail Safe Planning: Because Failing to Plan is Planning to Fail!"

> "Succession Planning for the Rest of Us!'

All very positively received books and instrumental in helping privately-owned business leaders create more success in their businesses.

<u>Paramount Business Development clients</u>. You all know who you are, and many of you have experienced the process of building a high-performance team at some level, some of you in a very detailed manner! While you do not realize it, you all are our inspiration. Everything we do is for you! You are what motivates us and makes us feel the urge to perform at a higher level daily for you! Thank you!

Cheryl, my (Rick's) wife, my love, my daily inspiration! You are always a steadfast believer and a constant steady supporter. Without you, many things would not be possible. Thank you for always being there!

My (Bill's) family, especially my lovely wife, Rita who has always believed in me and supported whatever I chose to do. Thank you! Love You! My three children who have always supported me and have always shown their love, respect, and pride towards me. Thank you! Rick for always showing tough love. Thank you!

And in remembrance, Coach Thom Finn. Coach Thom was a great colleague, great coach, and a great friend. He always urged us to do more and perform at a higher level.

Chapter 1

The Business Case for A High-Performing Team

You have taken the plunge and gone into business. There are many reasons why one starts a business or buys a business; they want to be their own boss, they believe they have a hobby that they can turn into a business, they feel they can do it better than who they work for now, etc.

If you have been in business for a while, or even if you are just starting out, your goal is to grow that business (and we have a framework to help you do that). To do that you will need employees i.e., a team. Hiring and leading employees takes a different set of skills which you may or may not have. In this book you will learn leadership skills, how to build your team, how to hire the best employees out there, and how to become a business that will attract good people.

First, let's start with some basics. You need to establish your company's culture. The five foundational basics that we discuss in establishing a culture when we teach strategic planning are: Vision, Core Values, Core Purpose, Core Why, and BOHAG. Without a solid foundation it will be hard to attract the right people to help you grow your business. Let's briefly review each of these areas.

Vision - An aspirational description of what a company would like to accomplish or achieve in the mid-term or long-term future. It is intended to serve as a clear guide for choosing current and future choices of action.   It should inspire and enroll. Every company needs a vision statement. It concisely tells everyone, including your team, where this business is headed and what you want it to be when it "grows up."

Next, you must decide what your values are as the owner/leader of the company. What are values? Values are a person's or business' principles or standards of behavior; one's judgment of what is important in life. You need to establish your values so you can establish the values by which you and your employees are going to run your company. Your values and your company values need to be synergistic and congruent. Values start as one word and then are explained in a short sentence or two. An example of a value word would be enthusiasm. We are enthusiastic about our company, our product, and our clients.

Company values set you apart from competition and give you a rallying point for your team. It will attract the people with similar values to become a part of your team. Strong company values will also lead to greater client retention and thus lead to greater profits.

From your values, determine your core values. Core Values are the most fundamental and most important values held by an individual or company. These core values are the guiding principles that dictate behavior and action.

Many companies focus on creating a mission(s) statement(s) for their company. This is okay. However, in today's world the 'mission statement' has become quite mutated, overused, and over exaggerated. We, today, prefer a simpler way that breaks it down into more usable, more meaningful, sub-segments. We simply break it down to your core purpose and your core why.

Core Purpose – this is a concise statement of what specifically you do as a company, or why you exist. An example could be: "to provide gourmet coffee to the discerning consumer." This example says exactly what you do, and who you do it for.

The need for a core purpose statement is to let the world know why your company exists. It provides your identity. It also performs the task of keeping you and your company on a well-defined path.

Core Why – this is a statement about why you do what you do. This tells the world, and your employees, why you are relevant and why you are focused on your core purpose. In the coffee example, a core why could be: "to use our extensive knowledge of the variety of high-quality coffee beans to create premium coffee drinks for our customers."

Finally, is your BOHAG; your Big Ole' Hairy Audacious Goal. The simplest definition is if you were given unlimited time, resources, and nothing out of bounds, what would you like to see your business accomplish? If your company is a residential security and protection company, a BOHAG may be to have your system in every home in America.

These are foundations in creating your company culture. A company culture represents a way of thinking, behaving, and working that exists in a place or organization. An organization's culture should be deliberate and reflect the vision, values, core purpose, core why, and BOHAG of the company. By putting these foundations on paper, your culture will evolve and it will allow you to attract and retain quality people, detect employee engagement problems, get everyone speaking the same company language, and get everyone working toward the same company vision.

Now that foundations are in place, you need to start growing your team. There are 7 keys to building a high-performance team.

Keys to A High-Performance Team ...

1. **Strong Leadership**
2. **Clear Communication**
3. **Inspiring Vision**
4. **Rules of the Game**
5. **Action Plan**
6. **Effective Delegation**
7. **100% Engagement**

PARAMOUNT
Business Development, Inc.

We will further develop each of these areas in subsequent chapters. We will spend a lot of time on each section to give you a better direction to develop your team, specifically leadership, helping you to become a better leader of your team and business.

Chapter 2

Key Number 1: Strong Leadership

Attributes of a Strong Leader

First, let's examine the mindset of a good leader. A leader needs to always be above the line, as pictured below. Leaders take ownership and are accountable and responsible for their actions and the performance of their team. They never blame anyone or make excuses, and they are never in denial or deny their actions. Sarcasm should also never be exhibited by leaders because it can be misconstrued and send the wrong message. It is a choice to always play above the line and leaders need to always make that choice.

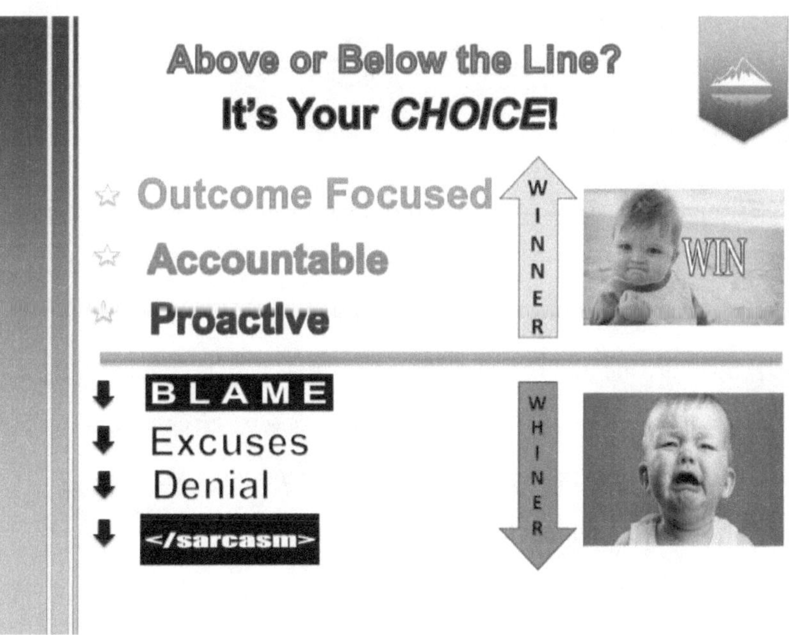

There is a distinct difference between being a manager and being a leader. The definition of leadership is the process of influencing others to achieve the organizational goals. Leadership is an interaction between the leaders, the followers, and the situation. The manager says, *"Go!"* The leader says, *"LET'S*

GO!" The leader knows the way, shows the way, and goes the way. Below is a chart comparing the difference between being a leader and being a manager.

Leader Vs. Manager

Leader	Manager
- Innovate	- Administer
- Develop	- Maintain
- Inspire	- Control
- Have long-term view	- Have short-term view
- Ask what and why	- Ask how and when
- Originate	- Imitate
- Challenge statues quo	- Accept the status quo
- Do the right things	- Do things right

Managers have people who work for them and leaders have people who follow them and work with them. A manager uses their mind and body to get things done because of their position over their subordinates. Leaders also use their mind and body, but they include their heart and spirit as well in the creation of high-performance teams. They genuinely want everyone to succeed and accomplish the company goal, as well as their own individual goals. Having heart and spirit is what gets people to follow and perform.

The Eight Core Leadership Competencies

There are eight core leadership competencies that are inherent in being a strong leader and are at the heart of every great leader. There are additional competencies that could be added to round this out to ten, twelve, fifteen, etc. However, the eight presented here are the foundation of every great leader. While some leaders may rise without each one of these eight, their leadership will not be sustainable in the long run.

The foundation of the great leadership competencies is **Integrity.** Integrity is simply doing the right thing when no one is watching. All great leaders are honest and highly ethical. To gain people's trust and have them follow you, you must learn and exhibit integrity very early on in assuming your leadership role. Remember to always be above the line in your own behaviors and actions.

Never go below the line and play the blame game. If things go wrong, leaders are accountable for their actions as well as their team's actions and results.

Great leaders have a **Vision**, another key attribute and pillar competency. Think of some great business leaders over the years; Ray Kroc of McDonald's, President Kennedy putting a man on the moon by the end of the decade, Sam Walton of Wal-Mart, Jack Welch of General Electric, and Bill Gates of Microsoft. All of them had a strong and inspiring vision of what they wanted to accomplish or what they wanted the company to look like. Vision is basically what you see your business becoming, your end game. The best visions are those that enroll and inspire your team. What are you doing to move your business closer to your vision, the higher purpose that inspires and enrolls your team?

Another pillar competency is **Passion.** All great leaders are passionate about their company, their vision, their team, and what they see them accomplishing as they move toward the vision. President Ronald Reagan wrote a book on leadership and was passionate about our country. Steve Jobs of Apple was very passionate about computers and their capabilities. Lee Lacocca Chrysler, author of "Where Have All the Leaders Gone?" was passionate about getting things done, and about leadership.

As a leader, you must know your why. Why do you do what you do, and what are you passionate about? Your passion should exude from you and your employees. It should be almost palpable.

Great leaders must be great communicators. **Communication** is key in any organization and a critical part of the business process. You as the leader must communicate so that everyone understands where you are going and why. Some examples of great communicating leaders include President Ronald Reagan, Martin Luther King, Roger Penske, and Prime Minister Winston

Churchill. They enrolled and inspired their constituents. What you need to communicate and knowing the best way to communicate it to the team is critical to successful communication. You need to be consistent with your communication to your team and make sure they receive the communication as it was intended. Most of the time you cannot over communicate. A key part of being a good communicator is being a good listener. You need to listen to team members with an open mind and take suggestions and criticism positively and use that information to make better decisions going forward.

Another key competency is **Commitment.** All great leaders are committed to their cause and their beliefs. Some examples are Bill Ford of Ford Motor Company, Mayor Rudy Giuliani, and Arthur Blank of Home Depot. To quote Sam Walton, "Commit to your business. Believe in it more than anyone else does."

You demonstrate your level of commitment by the hours you spend at work and what you work on when you're there. Are those hours productive and spent working on moving your business forward? How many hours per week do you spend on your business and committing to move it toward your vision? Do your employees know what you are really committed to?

Great leaders also need to have **Courage.** Often, you as a leader must head out on an unknown path. To embark on a new path or a change in direction can cause fear, not totally knowing what the possible outcome(s) could be. Remember though that fear is just **False Expectations Appearing Real.** You still must be willing to take the risk. Two leaders who have courage are Elon Musk of Tesla and Mark Zuckerberg of Facebook.

Look what has happened because of having the courage to take a risk. What could having courage to take a risk do for you company? Are there changes you could make? What new directions could you take your company? What is holding you back? Do you need more skills, data, or confidence to move forward? If the answer is yes, then you need to do what is necessary to gain the attributes needed to give you the courage to take the risks that will move your company forward.

Respect is another key competency that all good leaders must have. However, as the old saying goes, "Respect is earned not given." Oftentimes leaders expect respect without first giving it. Trust is important for the team to have in their leader because without it there is no basis for progress and the team will not be engaged and follow. In the military it is easy to lead because of your rank, but some leaders who earned the respect of their troops and the public were Collin Powell, US Army and Secretary of State, Norman Schwarzkopf, US Army General, and Dwight Eisenhower, US Army General and President of the US.

What have you done to earn the respect of your team? Do they know your vision and passion? Showing your courage and loyalty is very important in gaining the respect of your team. Walking the talk is important. Investing in and promoting your team helps build trust and will also help gain their respect. Successful leaders have successful track records and results which the team notices and in turn makes them want to follow. To gain respect from your team and peers you need to be a good listener, as discussed in communication. Listen to what they have to say and be able to take criticism.

Lastly, great leaders have **Humility.** Leaders should be humble and not have enormous egos. While some amount of ego is good, a little too much is too much. Leaders need to give credit where credit is due and realize that their success is dependent upon the team doing their jobs and what is expected of them. A good leader always puts the needs of another person before their own and thinks of others before themselves. They rarely draw attention to themselves and they also acknowledge when they are wrong.

Emotional Intelligence

Great leaders have ample amounts of humility. Usually what is considered part of that humility is emotional intelligence. Emotional intelligence is about understanding your emotions and the emotions of others. Growing up during the ice ages of leadership we were often taught not to worry about other people's emotions. However, in recent years, or at least since the mid-90s, it has been learned that emotional intelligence of a leader is often the critical linchpin of whether employees are motivated by or stay engaged with leaders.

We are practitioners of the Genos International Emotional Intelligence model. While this book is not about emotional intelligence, it is about building high-performance teams, and no discussion about high-performance teams would be complete without talking about emotional intelligence. The model for emotional intelligence contains 6 basic elements according to the Genos International model.

The first element is self-awareness, i.e. being aware of yourself and your emotions. Part of this first element is learning how to stay in control of your emotions as a leader, especially when things get messy. If you are not in control of your own emotions, how well will your team members trust you? It is often seen that people who have low self-awareness also have emotional instability. That instability will defeat your leadership.

The second element is awareness of others. A leader that is connected to his or her people and considers their feelings demonstrates a high level of awareness.

On the contrary, a leader who is not connected to his or her people and doesn't consider their feelings will have a very hard time leading them.

The third element is authenticity. Earlier we discussed integrity. Integrity and authenticity are very tightly intertwined. As a leader, being authentic is crucial and what it really means is walking the talk and being genuine.

The fourth element of emotional intelligence is emotional reasoning. Emotional reasoning means that when you are making decisions and plotting the course for the next actions for your company, you are also thinking about the responses and the emotions of others that will be affected by your decisions. This doesn't necessarily mean that you're going to make different decisions, it just means that you're going to consider other feelings than your own and it may alter the way you deliver your message.

The fifth element of emotional intelligence is self-management. This relates to self-awareness in element one. Self-management is about managing yourself, your emotions, your actions, and how you live out life each day in working with your team. It also means that you're in control, you're aware of yourself, and you're guiding your own behaviors based on what is needed for your company and your team.

The sixth and final element of emotional intelligence is inspiring performance. Managers demand performance and control performance. The core difference is leaders inspire performance. True leadership is about motivating, influencing, and inspiring performance.

Leadership Presence

All leaders must command a presence so that the team wants to follow them. We often talk about "how you show up." How you show up can entail several things, i.e. how you dress, how you speak, your mannerisms, your vocabulary, etc.

Not long ago we were working with a leader of a professional business services company that was having issues with his leadership presence. While he was the top leader and 50% owner of the company, his employees had very little respect for him. However, he usually showed up later in the morning, dressed like he was headed to the beach, and usually acted very nonchalant about everything. Do you see it?

Industry Knowledge

For your team to follow you, there is some basic knowledge that you need to have. You must have a knowledge of the industry in which you are working. If you were brought in from the outside because of your success and other skill sets you possess, you need to get up to speed on your new industry very quickly.

There are many ways to do this. Every industry is rife with periodicals and industry associations. The best way to learn a new industry is to get involved. Many industries have trade associations that look out for its constituents. This may be through government action, innovation, research, etc. The key to learning an industry is to read and get involved.

Financial Statements

Understanding financials is critical if you want to be able to successfully lead your company. You don't have to know how to create the reports, but you need a basic understanding of a balance sheet, an income statement, and a cash flow statement. Financial statements are the "language of business." If you lack proficiency in this area, there are many sources available to obtain this knowledge, but you must obtain it.

These key financial statements, as well as some other KPI measurements, are your scoreboard. They tell you how your company is doing and are fundamental in leading and making decisions going forward.

Critical Business Skills

Beyond financial statements, there are often critical business skills that are very important to the top leader of a company. That's not saying they must possess all these skills, but for the skills that they don't possess they must have someone on their inner team that does. Take marketing for example. The top leader of a company does not have to be a marketing expert, but if they are not strong in marketing, the most important thing is to have someone on the executive team that is. While the actual functions in this case could be outsourced, there must be somebody on the team that knows enough about marketing to make the appropriate decisions. We could go on and on about a list of critical business skills, but that is unnecessary and beyond the scope of this book. What is important to remember is that there are critical business skills and if you don't have them, make sure you hire appropriately to make up for this.

Not long ago we were working with a business leader who had some critical weaknesses in their skill set. Rather than admit these weaknesses, this business leader chose to try to bluff and convince everybody on the team that he had those skills. However, in working with this leader for a relatively short period of time, the other employees soon found out that the leader had no skills in certain areas despite his assertion that he did. So, not only did the lack of leadership skills torpedo the leader in several ways, what was more severely damaged was this leader's integrity. It was game over.

Planning

Planning is one of the key jobs of a leader. Poor planning will yield mediocre results at best for your company. Being able to set a course with input from the team is fundamental leadership. You, your key people, and your team's input need to establish the plan to successfully achieve the goals and results you want for the company. Then you need to see that the plan gets executed and adjustments are made, as necessary.

Your Dress Code

Long gone are the days of "every business leader must wear a suit!" Thankfully. The best advice is that a leader must always dress appropriately based on the situation. First impressions are key in demonstrating leadership. In today's business world you need to dress and appear however appropriate for your industry and/or the audience to which you may be in front of or presenting to.

Feel the Pulse

A leader needs to always be aware of all that is going on through information he or she has received from direct reports, competitive intelligence, or other outside sources. A good leader must be able to influence the direction of the company based on the information received. The leader, as stated earlier, must be accountable for results. Positive results are derived from the execution and continued monitoring, tweaking, and influencing of a good plan by the leader and leadership team to ensure company success.

Power Base

Good leaders establish a power base of go-to people that can help better strategize and create or implement the plan. This power base may come from within the company, the industry, synergistic industries, outside vendors, or other professionals that can be relied on as a sounding board for advice. A leader must not only maintain a good power base but should also always be looking to build that power base with other competent professionals that can continue to help grow the company and move it closer to the company vision.

As an extension of power base, many leaders of privately-owned businesses establish their own advisory board. This advisory board is usually made up of individuals with specific skills that help the leader have a dispassionate view of their business and make the right decisions for the business. Often the leader is too involved on a day-to-day basis to really see a clear picture of his or her business and the advisory board provides great insight and advice on how to grow and develop the company.

Engaging and Mobilizing Your Team

To become a respected and strong leader you must be able to engage and mobilize your team. If your team doesn't see you as a leader then it will be very difficult to lead them. What do you think your employees think about you? Would they view you as competent, committed, having integrity, character, and credibility? Do they know you are committed to their success? Do you have their respect even though you may not make the most popular decisions? Will they see that you admit your mistakes, that you go first and set the example, and that your words always match your deeds? If you aren't sure how they will respond to those questions and ideals, perhaps you need to survey them.

A survey will give you the information you need to improve any weaknesses you may have so that you can be more engaged and get the respect you want and deserve. You especially need to know what specific people reporting to you think, and what you need to do to earn their respect and the right to lead. Is there a behavior or attitude you could quickly change that would help you earn that right to lead?

You can no longer manage a team or "them" anymore, you need to manage and lead individually. Get to know your team- especially direct reports. List your employees from top to bottom and characterize their value and growth potential by percentile. What do you know about your employees/team members? It is important to know as much about your employees as you can.

Examples of things you should know about them are their career and personal aspirations; their motivators and values; any special talents, gifts, or skills; how they communicate; and what developmental needs they may have. The more you know about your employees, the better you can engage and lead them. There are many assessments we can supply that your team members can take for you to learn more about them. For each employee, based on the above factors, come up with the messages they need to hear from you to keep them engaged and mobilized. There are many types of messages you can give but they need to be specific to the employee. Always ask, "What support do you need from me?" Never abdicate.

To fully engage and mobilize employees, they need to know what their role within the organization is. You need to set clear expectations: what is expected of them; when they will receive feedback; what they may need to change as well as what support they will receive; etc. When team members exceed their expectations, you need to recognize and acknowledge them with their preferred form of acknowledgement. You do this by having a reward system in place. By properly acknowledging and rewarding employees they will continuously try to improve and become more loyal. Your goal should be to continually develop your employees for advancement and to become future leaders in your organization, therefore it is important to know your employees and engage them regularly.

Leadership Dashboard

 Many leaders can become overwhelmed and have difficulty focusing on what is important. Sometimes leaders believe that their team or organization isn't as focused as it should be. A tool that can be very helpful to keep a leader focused is called a Leadership Dashboard. In the interest of following the KIS method of "Keeping It Simple," a dashboard should be a one-page document to keep you focused on moving things forward. Let's go over some key things you should include on your dashboard.

The board should begin with a vision. Where do you see yourself and your organization in 3-5 years? The next item on the board should be you and your organization's mission(s), as stated earlier, you and your organization's purpose and the clients you serve.

Another key reminder on the leadership dashboard is your values. You need to have some non-negotiable core values for yourself. These values need to be lived, and your team and clients need to see how you live them.

Your organization should also have non-negotiable core values that are congruent with yours. They don't need to be identical, but they do need to be compatible or it will be a never-ending source of conflict and poor demonstration. These must also be lived and demonstrated by your team so that your clients know what you are about.

The dashboard should reflect your top three goals so you can measure performance. Ideally you should have 3 goals for the success of your career and 3 goals for the success of your organization, or the group that you lead within that organization. Too many "things" will divert a leader from getting duties done in a timely manner which can hinder growth of both the leader's career and the growth of the organization. Goals should always be in the S.M.A.R.T format, meaning they should be **S**pecific, **M**easurable, **A**chievable, **R**esults-oriented, and **T**ime sensitive. As you or your organization achieve a goal, replace it with another one that will either enhance or improve your career or organization. If you need help with setting up your dashboard, contact us or visit our website.

All leaders need to build relationships to be successful, not only for themselves, but for their organization or area of responsibility. These relationships could be internal or external. These key relationships should be listed on the dashboard to ensure that contact continues to be a focus with them.

Managing Overwhelm

Leaders are usually pulled in many directions and that sometimes can be overwhelming. Managing overwhelm is very important in becoming a strong leader and will also allow you to maintain balance between your personal and professional life. There are many time management theories and practices out there that one can acquire, and they are all helpful.

The first and most important thing to know about yourself is what your "Time Vampires" are as stated in the book by Dan Kennedy, *"No B.S Time Management for Entrepreneurs"*. He writes, "Time Vampires will suck as much blood out of you as you permit. If you're drained dry by day's end, it's your fault."

• Inadequate Planning	• Meetings; especially without agendas
• Fires-Management by Crisis	• "Multi-Tasking"
• Telephone/email interruptions	• Email Notifications
• Attempt Too Much/Prioritization	• Paperwork
• Accessibility	• Unfinished Tasks
• Disorganization/Environment	• Inadequate Staff
• Ineffective Delegation	• Socializing
• Lack of Self-Discipline	• Confused Responsibility or Authority
• Inability to Say No	• Poor Communication
• Procrastination	• Inadequate Controls or Processes
• Avoiding important items	• Incomplete Information
• Administrivia	• Travel

Which of these time vampires do you see wasting your time? Think about strategies that can help correct or overcome them. Also, who else on your team can help change that behavior?

Evaluating Your Time Use

There have been many treatises on how to use your time more effectively. Covering any of those in detail would be a waste of time and out of the context of this book. However, we feel the most straightforward and valuable time analysis tool was depicted in *"The 7 Habits of Highly Effective People"* by

Stephen Covey. One of the most useful things from the book is the time target or matrix you can use to determine how to allocate your time appropriately.

Please refer to that book for details, but the main thought of his tool is relatively easy to grasp. Stephen Covey presents a four-quadrant tool for analyzing your time. On the vertical axis is level of importance: important or not important, and on the horizontal axis is the level of urgency: urgent or not urgent.

It is important to concentrate on the things that are most important, but also the things that are considered important but not urgent. Leaders need to constantly be focusing and promoting goals, thus constantly moving the business forward. That is why you need to be focusing on what we call the "big rocks" and staying within the quadrant of not urgent, but important.

If the activity isn't moving you closer to achieving a goal, you need to question the importance of doing it. Items that are not urgent but important is where a leader should spend most of their time.

Tasks considered urgent and important are demand items that need to be handled and cannot be delegated. A good example of this might be a service crisis at your largest client.

The other quadrants, not important but urgent and not important and not urgent, are areas that leaders can easily get sucked into becoming deluded and distracted and taking their eyes off what is truly important. By concentrating on the important items, it allows them to maintain balance not only in leading the company, but also between their professional and personal lives.

One thing to think about is the important or not important criteria. Please remember that an item or task might not be important for you as the top leader but be a very important item or task for someone lower in your organization. In this case, delegation becomes your friend!

5 Time Management Tools

There are many tools to help leaders make better use of their time. We will discuss 5 of them briefly. First and foremost, all leaders need someone to help keep them accountable as they keep everyone else on the team accountable. An assistant or gatekeeper can keep things of lower priority off the calendar, keep the leader focused, and can help set and maintain boundaries. Many leaders use a coach to help them prioritize and stay focused.

Tool #1: The first tool is to have goals and invest in planning. Most individuals don't have **S**pecific **M**easurable **A**chievable **R**esults-oriented **T**ime sensitive goals, or **SMART** goals as mentioned earlier**.** Establish your goals and then plan how you are going to achieve them. The 6 P's of Planning; **"Proper Prior Planning Prevents Poor Performance"** applies here.

Many people don't like to plan but planning properly can give you a valuable return on that investment, so invest in planning time. Plans start with goals, and goals determine the tasks that need to be done to accomplish the plans. Many correlated tasks are a plan.

Tool #2: Tool number 2 is to establish a default schedule. A default schedule is more than just a calendar with appointments and times. A calendar has appointments, meetings, sales calls, vacations, personal dates, etc. A default schedule includes a notation as to the importance of the event, whether the event has been confirmed or needs to be confirmed, etc. This allows you to determine the relevance of the events on your calendar immediately. To truly establish a default schedule, records of tasks and time spent on tasks needs to be completed periodically.

Once that is done, review those activities and determine which ones are priorities based on the time target and achievement of goals. Questions a leader should ask about the activities he or she is doing are; what is the strategic value of this activity, does it have to be done, does it have to be done now, who else could do it, does it have to be done perfectly, and how can I save time on this activity? With the schedule prioritized, you will have identified time gaps to be able to complete additional activities that enable you to move toward achieving your goals. It will take time to establish a default schedule and it will never be written in stone, but it is the foundation for many other time saving tools.

Tool #3: The third tool to help save time is setting "office hours." Some believe in an open-door policy and others believe in establishing office hours. Both concepts can peacefully co-exist. Office hours are dependent on how important the reaction needs to be. There are some things that may need immediate attention and may take precedence periodically, but that should not become the routine. You need to use office hours for the important and not urgent things that need to get done. This usually consists of planning, strategizing, and activities that move the organization forward to achieving company goals, or in other words, proactive work. It also often requires deep thought and concentration. A leader's office hours should be guarded. Once a default schedule is established, there will be adequate time for office hours, proactive work, and handling any other necessary obligations.

Tool #4: Tool number 4 is to develop a task list. Most people put together a to-do list, which is a start, but only half the battle. A task list relates to the plan and can be as aggressive or passive as needed to achieve the result within the expected time frame. An example of a to-do list item could be "Lose 30 pounds," vs. a task list item, "Exercise for 30 minutes Monday, Wednesday, and Friday". Having a task list and executing the tasks will continually move you toward goal achievement and in many instances accomplish a goal in less time.

Tool #5: The fifth tool of the toolset to help manage overwhelm is work/life balance. While this may sound like an impossible task, or a confusing term, work/life balance is a very important part of time management in a business leader's world. Most leaders only think of work and what needs to get done next. The result is their personal life, health, and family all greatly suffer. However, a strong leader realizes that having balance between work and their personal life is extremely important. We need this personal time in which to rest, to renew, to enjoy life with our family, and to regain focus. Plus, what's the point of having a successful business if it doesn't benefit you and your family?

Many leaders hire a coach to help them with the above items, especially with the task list, to help them accomplish the organization's goals. A great coach helps you maintain your focus and improve your organization while living a great life and enjoying all that it can bring.

A very good example is the poor work/life balance that I (Rick speaking here) had during the years that I was doing corporate turnaround work. I was very good and highly effective at what I did. It often encompassed working 60-90 hours per week, and often 7 days per week. This was exceptionally poor work/life balance. It was extremely costly to my family life and my personal health. Both of which I am still paying for today, nearly 15 years later.

Orientations and Attitudes of a Strong Leader

As stated earlier, leaders need to be of the proper mindset. It has often been written that a leader's mindset is the most important thing relative to organizational performance. We as business/executive coaches couldn't agree more.

Above the Line

Leaders must always stay above the line, be outcome focused, accountable, and proactive. While it is true that everybody occasionally slips below the line, the top leader must consciously observe themselves being below the line and very overtly get themselves back above the line to lead by example.

Taking the High Road

Leaders must always take the high road and walk the walk, not just talk the talk. As a leader it is often very tempting to have quick and snappy answers. Leaders that are too egotistical are most often going to follow this line of action. However, in most situations, it's better to take a moment, think, and compose a good answer in all situations.

Constant Promotion of Vision, Values, and Goals

The metaphor often used is that the top leader of an organization is like the cheerleader of a sports team. No matter what the odds, no matter what the score, the cheerleader is always being promotional for the sports team. The top leader must be the same way. They must hold steadfastly to the values and vision and let nothing pull them off course. They must also have a steadfast pursuit of the organization's current goals. Again, leaders lead by example.

Thinking Comprehensively

Leaders must be able to think comprehensively and look at all possibilities and listen to input from others with an open mind. Improvement needs to be constant, not only in the organization and the team, but also in the leader themselves.   Not only do leaders have to lead through change, many times they need to lead the change if it is in the best interest of the organization and the team.

6 Disciplines of Execution

A good methodology model to follow is the _"Six Disciplines of Execution"_ by Gary Harpst. However, for actual following and executing of the 6 disciplines, we offer a slightly modified version below:

- Focus on the most important goal
- Define strategies to achieve that goal
- Create a complete implementation plan
- Develop and keep a compelling scoreboard
- Create and maintain accountability
- Continually evaluate & adjust accordingly

While we could go into great detail about this topic, that is out of the scope of this book. However, if you would like to know more, please pick up a copy of Gary Harpst's book or contact Paramount Business Development.

A leader needs to engage the team and have them buy into the goals, so everyone is rowing in the same direction. While a leader oversees directing the setting of the goals for an organization, they must also make sure everything is in alignment including goals, processes, measurements, policies, technology, and people. A leader should also be able to identify and recognize misalignments and put measures in place to fix them. This discipline is all about organizing the team and business for improvement.

Leading Change

Leaders need to lead through change, as change is inevitable. It has often been quipped that the only thing in the world that is constant is change itself. If the leader is new to his or her organization, or is a recent promotion, setting the goals for the organization and getting the team in alignment is a must. However, the next most important step is to lead this change in the organization. Most leaders underestimate how difficult leading change in an organization is. An organization has a certain direction, a certain motion, and a certain speed. Changing anything about that requires effort. For that effort to be successful, the enormity of that effort must be clearly understood.

Leading change is out of the scope of this book in detail; however, leading change is all about changing the hearts and the minds of the employees in the organization. We propose that a series of alignment meetings to announce the goals and discuss them, as well as discuss the implementation plan derived above, is incredibly important to help you achieve your organizational goals.

Leading Performance Improvement

The next key step is to develop an implementation plan. Leading your team through the implementation plan is a great way to create buy in and create an understanding of executing a plan. The implementation plan needs to include who is going to do what, and by when. This starts up the accountability process. Another key point of leading performance improvement is to establish a compelling scoreboard. As citizens of the most sports crazy nation in the world, we all understand dashboards and scoreboards. Painfully, few of us have ever used them in business.

We spent a lot of time discussing the attributes of being a strong leader, which may be the most important aspect of building that winning team and becoming the employer of choice, but there are 6 more steps in building that winning team and culture that employees want to join.

Chapter 3

Key Number 2: Clear Communication

To attract people to a company or organization, a charismatic leader is certainly important, but your team and culture is equally important. Communication is a key component of building a successful team and culture and must constantly be worked at. Leaders must be great communicators. The existing and potential new team members should not only know what the leadership team is communicating but be able to understand it as well. One of the top problems we find in many organizations is communication.

The definition of true communication is *"the response you get"*. Therefore, if the response from a peer, subordinate, or superior is not what is expected or does not make sense, then the communicator must first look at how they are conveying the message.

As stated above, leaders need to be great communicators but everyone within an organization should also be able to communicate clearly and effectively. A communicator must think about what needs to be communicated, how to communicate it, how often to communicate it, and ascertain how the communications are being received and perceived. The question raised is, do you ever think there is over communication? We personally believe you communicate until told it is enough or you are consistently getting the response you expect.

Communication is a two-way process, **listening** and **speaking**. Please note that we listed listening first!

Listening: There are many key principles for being a good active listener. First, concentrate on the person that is speaking. Do not interrupt, judge, or multi-task. If you're not concentrating on the communicator, what are the chances you will be hearing what they are saying? Listen all the way through and try to understand their opinion, point of view, interest, or even aspiration. When there is a break, ask questions to make sure you understand and to signal to the communicator that you are listening.

Listen for opportunities to move things forward and for their feelings and emotions. Never let your mind wander or get distracted about what you want to say or ask next. Always be in the moment, listening intently so that you understand how they may feel and can say something that lets them know that. If appropriate, take notes and restate or review what was said for clarity. If taking notes, circle or highlight repeated items, as they may be significant. It is also important to pay attention to their body language so you can pick up on things that might not be said.

There are 3 modes of communication: words, voice, and body language. Studies have shown that words constitute 7%, voice 38%, _and body language 55%!_ To be a good active listener, one must pay attention to all three modalities. Many times, it is the voice volume or tone that will be more definitive than the actual words. The same is true with body language. Are they relaxed or do they fidget? Voice and body language can give the listener much more insight into the communication than just the words alone. Even in non-face to face communication such as phone calls, emails, or texts, one can get a sense of the type of communication.

Many attorneys, judges, and policemen will tell you that they watch the body language of the speaker more than they listen to the words. We will let you guess why. They will tell you that often a person's body language conflicts with their words. As a listener, when you notice this, you need to ask deeper probing questions to get a good understanding of what the speaker really means.

As a final note about listening, many will be endeared to a supervisor or leader that truly listens to them. Sadly, in our world there are too many people that talk and too few people that listen. The most motivating and relationship building thing you can do for your team is to simply listen to them. All the way through.

Speaking

Speaking is *believed* to be more important of the two when it comes to communicating. When people think about communication, the first thought that comes to their mind is speaking. But as we mentioned earlier, speaking is really the 2nd in the two key parts of communication. In our context we will refer to speaking as in verbal communication. Many of the principles can also be related to written, whether that be emails, texts, etc.

Leaders and others in any organization need to verbally communicate daily and there's a good chance that they need to improve their speaking communication skills. There are many avenues in which to improve your speaking, both personally and publicly. For more about speaking skills, please tap into the many resources that are available.

While this is not a book on speaking, there are many points that we do want to cover that you will not find in a typical book, webinar, or class on speaking. We will break communication into a few vital segments:

- Be the message
- Be authentic
- Set the tone
- Communication approach
- The 5 segments of communication planning
- The rule of 3's
- Communicate to move critical items forward

- Crucial conversations, and
- Conflict resolution

Be the Message

Communicators must _"Be"_ the message. The following questions may help you understand where there is potential for improvement in being the message:

- How do you communicate the crucial goals, results, etc. and the progress?
- How do your behaviors match your communication?

As mentioned earlier, there are many modes of communication. You need to choose the mode that correlates with the importance of your message. As leaders, we are often like goldfish in a bowl at the county fair. When you get them home, you find the goldfish are often much smaller out of the bowl due to the magnification effect of the small bowl. Due to that magnification effect of our Leadership Fishbowl, everything we do is highly visible and highly scrutinized. Our team watches us very closely and judges our communication based on our behaviors. "Do we walk the talk?"

- How much of your information do you give?

When communicating, it is often a challenge to judge how much information to give. Too little will make an incomplete message and too much will turn them off or put them to sleep.

- How important is it for you to be right?

This is a critical question. Many leaders just <u>must</u> <u>be</u> <u>right</u>- even when they aren't! You may need to ask yourself, "Is it more important to be right, or more important to get my message across and be respected?"

—   What is your observable focus?

Back to the fishbowl. Most team members will notice what we are focused on and follow our lead. This is a good point on leading by example. We must demonstrate what is important through our actions.

—   How do you behave under pressure?

It has been interesting to watch our state and national leaders through this recent Covid-19 crisis. They are certainly under tremendous pressure and it shows. Some are doing amazingly well while some are falling apart. How calm, thoughtful, and agile on your feet are you when under pressure?

—   When things don't go well, how do you react?

The most telling part about you as a leader is how you respond when things do not go well. What do you do? Do you lose your cool? Do you get short and tense with people? Do you start belittling others? Many leaders build their respect up during normal times only to lose it all when things do not go well.

—   How do you accept your shortcomings?

How well do you admit when you are wrong, or when you didn't get something done on time? Many think they can hide it, explain it away, blame it on others, or even deny it. All bad moves! As a leader, you earn a tremendous amount of respect when you admit and own up to your shortcomings.

—   How do you react to other's failures?

Everyone has moments of failure. Everyone. Even your "A players". How do you handle it? One of the better leaders we know says they have big dumpsters in their parking lot to handle all their failures! His point is that he, and all his team, makes failures and that is okay. It is part of learning and growing.

— How do you support those who fail?

What do you do? Like a kid playing baseball, you should help them get back up, brush them off, and tell them to get back out there in the game. One leader Rick has worked with explains it this way, "It is okay to make a mistake; it is not okay to keep making the same mistake!"

— Do you spend the most time with super performers, or the laggards? … What does that say about you?

An old management adage was to always spend time with the poor performers in hopes to help them improve. This is okay, but wouldn't it be better to spend more time with the super performers to help them be better? If you do not spend time with the super performers, what does that show them?

— How do your behaviors support your goals, etc.?

Many leaders miss this point. It is said that John D. Rockefeller believed that if anything was significantly important to you as a leader, you should spend a good amount of your time focusing and working on it. What do you spend most of your time on? It is an observable behavior that your team sees.

— How do you react to your superiors when things do not go well? Who takes the heat?

Go back and reread the comments about accepting and owning up to your shortcomings. The same goes for your superiors. Blame someone else once and everyone notices and is on guard. Do it twice and you just lost your ability to lead and will never be trusted again.

- What % of time do you spend on the goals?

Please reread the above about John D. Rockefeller.

- What employee behaviors do you reward?

This is a very in-depth topic. Also consider what a reward is. Is it time? Attention? An opportunity for lunch? Drinks after work? We could write a separate book about this topic alone. Just be aware that your actions are watched closely. There are many different opinions on what constitutes a reward.

- What employee behaviors do you ignore?

This is very connected to the above topic. For high performers, recognition and rewards are very important. Most are intuitive and are very aware of when they are being ignored. Do not underestimate the power of ignoring a team member whose behaviors are not conducive to team performance.

- What employee behaviors do you punish?

Yes, it's sad to say but this is important too. We will discuss this later in the book, but frequent performance planning sessions are highly recommended. Part of this process is having clear communication about behaviors that need to be changed or stopped. Punishment should never be meant to be punitive, but more so encouragement for change.

Be Authentic

What does authentic mean? What is authenticity? This is not a tricky word with an obscure meaning. It is very straightforward and means exactly what the word suggests. It means genuine, unquestionable, true to one's word, nature, and beliefs.

Anyone who is a communicator, particularly a leader, needs to be authentic. Many communicators and leaders fail because of a lack of authenticity. To be authentic as a communicator, one needs to ask questions like: Who is not being held responsible? What goals or tasks are sliding? What conflicts are being avoided? And what lies are being perpetrated and are being ignored? As the communicator/leader, are you walking the walk or just talking the talk? If there isn't authenticity, the team and others will see right through you and they will not be listening. In turn, you will lose all credibility and respect.

Set the Tone

One of the key responsibilities of a leader is to set the tone for their organization or their objective. Setting the tone is the clear prerogative of the leader and is necessary in determining the overall tenor of the organization.

For example, a leader can set a fast and frenetic tone which will move the organization forward in a very fast fashion but will also wear it out soon. Another example could be the slow, steady, and thoughtful approach which oftentimes sets an organization up on a steady path but can sometimes delay results and remove the sense of urgency. A leader needs to think about what tone he or she needs to set for every given initiative they may make.

While this topic may not make sense quickly, as executive coaches, we can go into an organization and get a sense of the tone that the leader has set by spending a little bit of time with the team members. As a leader it may not seem like setting the tone is having an effect, but subtle changes in setting the tone can have a dramatic effect on how the organization behaves and responds. It is important to put thoughtful time into considering this before communication on any major initiative.

Communication Approach

The approach that you use for communication is important and should be considered when speaking to others about important topics. The approach may change based on the audience or the topic.

There are 6 basic approaches to communicating. There is the intellectual approach, or **left-brain approach,** which utilizes the left portion of the brain. It is used when you want to convince the team through logic and communicate facts that only you have but are important to the listeners. This approach is best used when presenting data, facts, and logical approaches to solving problems. It is best when speaking to highly technical people such as accountants, lawyers, engineers, and doctors.

Another approach is the emotional approach, or **right-brain approach,** which utilizes the right portion of the brain. This approach goes beyond logic and gets the receivers of the communication to tap into their emotions by using teachable moments, stories, and metaphors. It is more effective when communicating topics that are very subjective and emotional. It is typically used among people who are less technical but more on the creative, artsy, liberal side of things.

The third kind is **the gut approach,** or fear approach. Leaders and communicators often use this approach when negotiating a settlement, presenting a discipline action, or forming a contract by using things in their control to leverage what may be important to the team or others involved in the communication. In this approach the speaker is often leaning on their source of positional or leadership power to effect the change or outcome they are seeking.

The opposite approach would be **the heart approach,** or passion approach. To be truly effective the communicator may need to show some vulnerability which may mean admitting shortcomings or asking for help. In this approach, the leader needs to really delve into and stir the passion of the followers or the audience. A good example of this is President George W. Bush's communication in pursuing al-Qaeda in Iran and Afghanistan. Due to the emotions of the topic, the American people had a real passion for justice in this endeavor.

The next approach is **the spirit approach.** The leader shares their vision, common beliefs, and experiences and asks others to build on and buy into the vision.   This approach is used to re-energize the team or to get people excited about a new project, even if the steps are currently unknown. A great example of this is a basketball coach getting his/her team fired up to go out and win a tournament such as the NCAA March Madness tournament.

The final approach is **the legs approach.** This is best described in the fight or flight context. It is used in situations where a withdrawal or retreat is the best option. An example of this is when you need a certain activity or meeting stopped before things get worse. Sometimes it is best to withdrawal and come back to the topic or problem at another time.

The 5 Segments of Communication Planning

When planning communication, it can be broken down into 5 basic segments:

> Who is being communicated to? E.G.: the team, an individual, a client, etc.?

> What is the communication vehicle? E.G.: a hallway conversation, an offsite retreat, email, phone call, social media.

What is the purpose of the communication? E.G.: acknowledgement, ideas, training, inspiring, socializing, etc.

What gets communicated? E.G.: results, strategies, asking for help, initiatives, values, vision, missions, etc.

What is the communication frequency? Frequency is determined by the group and what is being communicated. Some items and groups need regular communication and some need less. Sometimes important items need to be reiterated several times to get the point across thoroughly.

The Rule of 3's

To keep communication clear, simple, focused, memorable, and powerful, a good rule of thumb is the Rule of 3's. The Rule of 3's states that concepts or ideas presented in 3's are essentially more interesting, more enjoyable, and more memorable. It's no accident that the number three is prevalent in well-known stories: The Three Little Pigs, The Three Musketeers, or The Three Wise Men. In any communication, using the Rule of 3's will keep the communicator focused, the message focused, and the communication memorable to the listeners.

Leaders often have many things that they want to communicate to their followers, or their audience. However, in considering that you want to keep things memorable for creating action and buy in, it's often better to limit the amount of information that is communicated.

There are occasionally times when our communication effort needs to contain more than three things. However, in those rare instances, a good approach is to provide a handout. And if it is a complicated topic where there are seven or eight things that need to be communicated, the best approach is to provide a handout with bullet points. The thing that you must remember as a communicator is how important it is that the message be received well, understood, and retained by the audience.

Communicate to Move Critical Items Forward

Leaders frequently need to move critical items forward. Individuals, or the team, can become negative, apathetic, resistant, or just stuck in the status quo if they are not constantly enrolled, engaged, and inspired.

Good leaders must have the ability to steer people towards more productive conversations that will excite them and keep them engaged. Some areas that can reinvigorate the team may be reiterating the vision and the goals and giving positive updates on progress. Another reinvigorating communication could be discussions about ideas, opportunities, and possibilities, i.e. brainstorming. Most people love the freewheeling of brainstorming.

Sometimes we over analyze and get paralysis by analysis. Leaders can create excitement by asking for input and actively listening to what team members have to say. People love to give input, especially if they believe it is being listened to and well received. It is powerfully motivating to see your ideas and critiques making a difference.

Another way to move critical items forward is to have a communication about important initiatives that need to be accomplished. Ask your team how they think the initiative could be accomplished and what they could do to accomplish it. Let them help set a course of action for achievement of the initiative and then celebrate when that achievement is accomplished. Recognizing the team will keep them engaged and inspired, thus continuing to move critical items forward.

Crucial conversations

Perhaps a simpler definition of crucial conversations is conversations that most people do not like to have. The first thing that comes to mind is performance reviews. Performance reviews are something that we all know need to happen on a periodic basis, but in nearly nine out of ten companies that we become familiar with, they are not done.

Another example is disciplinary conversations. Often, disciplinary conversations are not had until the leader blows up and is ready to fire the employee. And that is not productive.

A good way to explain crucial conversations is to talk about what constitutes a crucial conversation. Examples are listed below:

> Performance reviews
>
> Consistent unacceptable behavior
>
> Providing honest feedback on poor performance
>
> Disciplinary meetings
>
> Holding team members accountable for results
>
> Discussions about goals not met
>
> Discussing taboo issues e.g. hygiene or attire
>
> Being able to say no
>
> Explaining tough options in the face of adversity
>
> And many more

Most people avoid these conversations because they are difficult and frequently ugly. However, a good leader must have the courage to address these crucial conversations to move the company forward. In the situations where these conversations are not occurring, it generally damages the organization, the team, and the results.

A good way to think about these crucial conversations is to think about just ripping the band-aid off. Once these conversations are taken care of, you will feel better as a leader and the organization will move forward.

How many crucial conversations are you avoiding from the list above?

Using Emotional Reasoning in Crucial Conversations

Using emotional reasoning is a helpful approach in planning a crucial conversation. This entails thinking about the audience that you will be speaking to as well as how they will receive their communication based on what you know about their personality and their emotions.

While it won't change the conversation in terms of what gets communicated, it will most likely greatly change how it's communicated. Taking into consideration the audience's point of view and their probable emotions will prepare you to better deliver the message so that it is better received.

A good example of this point is from the TV show the Big Bang Theory. In this show Sheldon often is correct in what he says but he's almost always wrong in how he delivers the message. If you've ever seen the show, you'll know what we are referring to. If not, check it out and you will quickly understand our example.

Conflict Resolution

Conflict is an omnipresent factor in the daily life of an organization. Conflict is natural and can be constructive if handled correctly. Contrary, if not handled in the correct manner, it can have bad effects and be costly. Conflict can present hard and soft costs to the company; results, careers, customers (both internal and external), the team, and other people, including the leader.

Resolution of conflicts mitigates all the negative issues that surround what is listed above. The quicker a conflict is resolved, the quicker things mend, and productivity returns to the team and organization. Resolving conflict will improve teamwork, improve morale, create a more positive environment, build better relationships, and relieve stress. Resolving conflicts takes leadership, patience, self-awareness, and above all else, excellent communication skills.

A good place to start in resolving conflict is to look at some of the possible underlying issues. Is having conflict a cultural norm? Is having conflict an expectation of the leader? Although it's sad, there are some organizations where conflict is just part of normal everyday life.

A great question to ask in resolving the conflict is, "What is the leader's point of view on this topic?" Is the leader motivated to resolve the conflict? If the leader is not motivated to resolve the conflict, then this becomes a moot point and a waste of time. We have worked with leaders who had the misguided thought that conflict created what they called "creative tension" and was good for the organization. We have yet to see a situation when this was true.

There are 2 keys in resolving conflicts. Key number 1 is how willing the communicator or leader is to resolve the conflict. Give it a number on a scale of 1 to 10 with 1 being not willing to resolve to 10 being very willing to resolve. List the things that may need to be given up to resolve the conflict. Some of those things may be being right, looking good to the team, being invulnerable, fear, etc. Key number 2 is what percentage of responsibility the leader or communicator is willing to take. Again, give it a number on a scale of 1 to 10 with 1 being not taking any responsibility to 10 being taking full responsibility.

 As Stephen Covey states, "seek first to understand, then to be understood". There are 2 things you must understand to successfully resolve conflicts.

Number 1 is the other person(s) position and point of view. Consider what the other person may say about the conflict. There may be past issues causing resentment that could be feeding into this current conflict. Think of the bright side or what becomes possible for the other person if the conflict is resolved. In other words, what may be their wants? Sometimes to resolve a conflict the leader or communicator may need to simply ask for the other person's point of view, make amends or apologize for previous transgressions, find common ground, or paint a compelling picture of how things could look upon resolution.

Number 2 is understanding the whole person, if possible. Try to understand their world at work and home. Look for areas of similarities and possibly what motivates them. Are their goals the same as yours? How can you possibly work together to help each other achieve these goals? There may be more commonality than either side realizes. Communicate in their style to make them more comfortable and possibly resolve the conflict easier. Always try to know as much about the person as possible to make it easier to find common ground to resolve the conflict. The next step in preparing to successfully resolve a conflict is determining the needs of the communicator or leader. What is needed from them to resolve the conflict and how flexible is everyone is willing to be. The leader or communicator must realize when they should stop worrying about being right and powerful and move the conflict forward to get results. The communicator or initiator of the resolution process must think about what request they may need to make of the other person, but still have a positive impact on them.

A second need to be considered by the leader or communicator is determining common ground on which resolution can be built. What are the motivations, goals, aspirations, and risk tolerance of both sides, professionally and personally? The more a leader or communicator knows about the key criteria and behaviors of the person in conflict, the easier resolving the conflict can be.

Below are some possible resolution strategies for conflicts:

- Ask for their perspective and build a win-win solution by being flexible. Be willing to listen and authentically include them.
- Apologize for a past issue and resolve it. Ask to move forward. Acknowledge them for their contributions, genuinely and without being manipulative.
- Tell them you want to resolve the conflict and ask, "what will it take?"
- Offer them thing(s) they want to create a truce or contract about working well going forward: negotiate a truce.
- Give up the need to be right, look good, get credit, or something else holding back the relationship.
- Make a request of them and be prepared to offer something in return.
- Share common ground and develop a sense of common purpose.
- Get a third party to interview them and bring you both together for a facilitated discussion.

There are a few quick strategies when dealing with conflict before and during the meeting you could employ:

- Never have the meeting or interaction if angry; cool down first.
- Always attack the problem or issue.
- Remember it's not personal.
- Focus on the issue, not your position on the issue.
- Always accept and respect differing opinions and work to develop a common agreement and a win-win resolution.

- Focus on areas of agreement, not disagreement, and never make assumptions about what the other person is feeling or thinking.
- Use your listening skills.
- Do not interrupt.
- Ask clarifying questions for understanding only.
- Always thank the other person for listening and participating.

When preparing to resolve a conflict, always plan for the worst and objections. Plan for the meeting; do not just "wing it." List possible objections that could occur. Think of the most appropriate response for each objection that is listed. There are certain things the leader or communicator may want to avoid saying based on the conflict or what they know about that person. Don't let the meeting spiral out of control. If necessary, call a time out to the meeting and agree to reconvene when everyone has had a chance to cool down and reconsider.

Creating a Communication Structure

The final topic to be discussed under the overall topic of clear communication is setting up a communication structure. It is important to set up a communication structure as part of that critical business process. One of the necessary tools prior to setting up a communication structure is having a clear organizational chart. While many different organizational structures have been implemented in companies large and small, the most successful, continuous organizational structure is that of a standard superior and subordinate organization.

The purpose of having a clear organizational chart is so that everyone knows where they stand in an organization, who works for them, and who they work for. A topic that is out of the context of this book is also having clear duties and responsibilities established for each person in that organizational chart for efficiency, completeness, and accountability.

Once the organizational chart is clearly understood, the next step is to set up a communication structure to keep all levels of the organization informed as to goals, priorities, and to do items. The communication structure will most likely include recurring meetings with certain groups i.e. an executive team with executive team meetings, a sales team with sales team meetings, etc. Sadly, many leaders think that because they know something that everybody in the organization should also know it. Of course, as few people are true mind readers, this is rarely the case. Information must be communicated.

The last piece of a good communication structure is to think about who should be in those regular standing meetings and how frequently they should be held. For example, on an executive team meeting it should be the top managers and the meeting should probably be held monthly; better yet, weekly. The idea of the meeting frequency is to establish a rhythm for that team.

Chapter 4

Key Number 3: Inspiring Vision

In Chapter 1 we talked about having an inspiring vision for the organization. An inspiring vision is often what really captivates and motivates the team. The usual problem is that many visions are either not communicated, or they are not inspiring. There are many examples of inspiring visions out there in the world.

A vision is simply where the organization sees itself in the future. We often jokingly say that it's what you want to be when you grow up. Ideally, a vision statement improves the organization's effectiveness and productivity because it motivates and guides everyone involved to work towards a shared vision.

The leader needs to make sure that his or her personal vision is in alignment with the vision of the organization. If the vision of the leader is not parallel with the vision of the organization, the chance of leading the organization toward realizing the vision will be very difficult, if not impossible.

A great planning process should include the team in a visioning exercise to establish a vision if there isn't one present, or review and refine the vision that is already in place. The vision will likely change over time as changes occur in the economy, technology, organization status, and our world in general. Reviewing the current vision is always a good idea to make sure it is still relevant. A vision statement should be general, (which allows it to survive, even in an unstable environment) short, precise, and clarify the organization's direction and purpose.

Examples:

To become the world's most loved, most flown, and most profitable airline.

-Southwest Airlines

Bring inspiration and innovation to every athlete* in the world. (*If you have a body you are an athlete)

- Nike

Next, the organization should establish a BOHAG, or Big Ole' Hairy Audacious Goal. Simply put, if an organization had unlimited time and money, what would be the Number 1 organization-wide goal that they would like to achieve? A BOHAG is created to focus an organization on a single mid-term or long-range goal which is audacious and a big reach!

Often, we do not know an organization's BOHAG as outsiders. But in the Southwest Airlines vision example above it would be easy to believe their BOHAG is to be the biggest airline in North America.

The next key step in keeping the team focused is to have goals that the organization wants to achieve. These should include 3 to 5-year goals, annual goals, and 90-day goals. Each level of goals should be congruent with the others and prioritized so that if only one gets accomplished, it will be the most important one.

The team must then be aligned with the vision, BOHAG, and goals of the organization. In bigger organizations the vision, BOHAG, and goals are commonly set by the leadership team. In smaller organizations all key team members can be involved in the alignment and planning process for the organization, but this is unusual. A team alignment meeting should be conducted to create a common understanding and buy-in. This ensures that the team aligns themselves with the vision, BOHAG and goals of the organization.

The importance of inspiring vision is to provide direction and focus for the organization and team. Key # 3 should be referenced on a regular basis to remind your team of where you are going and to engage, enroll and inspire them. Having an inspiring vision is one of the reasons people will want to work for you and it will also retain your good people. If you need help in establishing your goals and developing your plan, read **Fail Safe Planning** by Rick Munson (available on Amazon), visit our website, or call us to help you.

Chapter 5

Key Number 4: Rules of the Game

The next key in becoming an employer of choice is to establish the rules of the game, the rules of *your* game. Business is a sport, and you need to play for keeps. So, establish the rules for *your* game of business. One of the most important aspects of building a team is to build the right culture for that team to thrive in. You need to deliberately build a culture and live by that culture and set of rules to retain quality employees and attract quality employees.

Core Values

One of the first steps is establishing the organization's core values. What is the definition of a value? A value; a person's or business's principles or standards of behavior; one's judgment of what is important in life. Core values are the fundamental beliefs of a person or organization. The core values are the guiding principles that dictate behavior and action, without them it is very difficult to maintain the consistency of the organization. Core values are the foundation that an organization is built on and the glue that holds the organization together.

There are many reasons why core values are important. Core values set a company apart from competition by clarifying its identity. Companies that establish core values, identify with them, and promote them have a rallying point for their team. Living by the company's core values and continually reminding employees of them leads to less employee turnover as well as higher customer retention. A strong set of core values keep you doing business consistently. Most businesses with strong published core values show a higher profitability compared to those that don't.

Core values are powerful. They need to be memorable and can't be too long. They can't be platitudes. They must be unique to the owner's and organization's beliefs and must be actionable. Leaders must think, act, and live the core values by example. Everyone in the organization needs to be passionate about them and be willing to live them.

Core values can help unify the team, attract the best talent, and help set KPI's (Key Performance Indicators) for sales and marketing. They need to become part of the daily culture of the organization. Customers will align with the values of the organization and become loyal, quality customers. Core values must be connected and support the vision and goals of the organization.

There are some key steps to follow in establishing core values for an organization. First and foremost, the owner or leadership team must establish if they even want to be a values-based company or organization. As mentioned earlier, the organization's core values need to align with the personal values of the founder, owner, leader, or leadership team. A determination needs to be made as to who on the team should be involved in helping to select the core values that will drive the organization. One of the best ways to set core values is to brainstorm with key team members to see what is important to them and the team. Then the brainstorming group needs to prioritize and consolidate the list as to which core values they want to live by. Then short, memorable phrases or sentences about each value needs to be written to define it to the organization. The brainstorming group then presents the set of values to the rest of the team. Some examples of key values are integrity, trust, accountability, communication, balance, leadership, risk taking, positivity, cooperation, compassion, innovation, and many more.

There is no set number of core values an organization can have. However, the best advice is to keep the number of core values between 5 – 8 as too many values can be overwhelming. Keeping a relatively few core values makes them more memorable, and thus pertinent and actionable.

Core Value Examples:

Starbucks Coffee

With our partners, our coffee, and our customers at our core, we live these values:

- Creating a culture of warmth and belonging, where everyone is welcome.
- Delivering our very best in all we do, holding ourselves accountable for results.
- Acting with courage, challenging the status quo, and finding new ways to grow our company and each other.
- Being present, connecting with transparency, dignity, and respect.

Wawa Convenience Stores

- Value people
- Delight customers
- Embrace change
- Do the right thing
- Do things right
- Passion for winning

McDonald's

- Sustainable priorities
- Good food
- Good planet
- Our people & communities

Ford Motor Company

- Put people first
- Be curious
- Built Ford tough
- One Ford
- Play to win
- Create tomorrow
- Do the right thing

A final note about core values; they must be something you are willing and desiring to live by, to continuously promote, to thoroughly believe in, and willing to discipline those that do not subscribe to them. The final acid test of core values: "are you willing to fire someone that violates them?" Then, and only then, will you know you are serious about them.

On that note, how do you grow the adherence to your core values and hold your team accountable for them? How do you hold people accountable for performance? The answer to these two questions is very similar.

A great way to hold team members accountable for the core values is to give them a grade on how well they are living by and demonstrating them. During the performance review, create a check off system for each core value and rate people 1 – 5 on each one. A score of 1 would be poor and a grade of 5 would be excellent. When team members start getting graded on how well they live the core values, they will get the message.

Creating That High-Performance Culture

It is important to take some time to create the culture you want for the organization. The preceding core values are an important start. From even earlier, setting the tone is very important. But what else? What does it mean to be a high-performance culture?

The culture created and the one the team lives by needs to be outcome focused. Meaning that the team and organization is constantly moving the business forward on positive outcomes. By maintaining this focus, greater strides are made toward achieving goals and they are usually accomplished at a faster pace.

To be a high-performing culture, everyone in the organization must be "above the line" and be accountable. If every team member is above the line and accountable for their actions and their own results and holds others accountable, the organization will thrive. A spirit of accountability will lead to less errors and those errors that occur will be rectified in a timelier manner. There will also be less blame, excuses, and denial, which all detract from positivity and progress.

A high-performance culture is proactive, meaning anticipating what will happen instead of waiting for it to happen. The individual, team, or organization makes things happen rather than responding to things after the fact. Proactivity will keep the organization on the cutting edge of its industry and will maintain steady movement forward. By building a culture of go-getters, the organization will attract similar types of individuals and move at a faster pace than the competition.

Maintaining a high-performance culture takes significant work. An important element is employee planning systems. There are several parts of employee planning systems: organization charts, performance planning, development planning, career planning, performance pay systems, and effective discipline plans.

Organization Charts

An organizational chart is an important part of employee planning systems. A current organization chart is hopefully obvious, but for this discussion, the next step is the future organizational charts at points in the future such as 1, 3, and 5 years out. This allows all team members to see what opportunities there are within the organization and what they could aspire to. It also allows the top leaders to understand the talent needs for the future.

Everyone in the organization should be assessed as to where they are now. The leader should determine the fit of each person in the organization. He/she should be asking if this is the right person for the team. Further, is this person in the right position in the organization? Other questions, regarding the future organizational charts, are what training a team member could use to make them more valuable to the organization to fill roles in the future?

For an organization to be successful, it is extremely important to have the right people and in the right seats. If not, the organization will be lethargic, and it will be difficult to get things done successfully and timely. Sometimes organizations have good people who are just simply in the wrong seats.

Positional Agreements

Roles are general terms, and responsibilities are specifics. You need to have job descriptions, or as we prefer, positional agreements (PA) for all positions in the company. Positional agreements go beyond the standard job description by including the key performance indicators (KPI's) that their performance will be measured against. The key here is measurement of performance. If you need help developing positional agreements, contact us and we will be happy to help you.

Once the PA's are developed, communicate and review with each employee along with a current organizational chart. The organizational chart serves as a symbol of authority as well as a communication tree and is necessary for team members to know who is responsible for other areas.

Positional agreements have three implications. The first being strategic, which aligns your people with the vision and goals of the organization. The second is tactical, as these express the tools that need to be used and what needs to be accomplished in all areas of the employee's life cycle. The third is all the legal aspects of the PA. This implication isn't always needed but it will keep you in compliance with local and federal regulations. Creation of PA's require analysis of all current and future positions as well as the relationship of one position to another. If you don't have PA's in place now, make sure you get input and feedback from the people that are performing those duties now. Include all key elements of the position in the PA. There is nothing more critical to team success than well written PA's and the communication of them to the team with resultant expectations.

One of the goals here should be to eliminate duplication and confusion as well as any gaps in responsibilities. Imagine a team where multiple people are doing the same responsibilities and getting into conflict over it. This is not very efficient. The second case is responsibilities that do not get handled because they go unnoticed and slip under the radar.

Some Key Elements for a PA are:

> Job title and salary range
>
> Fair Labor Standards Act (FLSA) status
>
> Objectives and purpose for the position
>
> Reporting structure
>
> Duties and responsibilities
>
> Education/experience requirements
>
> Any other qualifications and specific skills required
>
> Work locations and conditions
>
> How the employee will be measured on basic responsibilities
>
> Standards of performance

The Performance Planning Orientation

As a leader or team member you are a communicator. The workplace disappointments need to be handled either by the leader or by a peer. Some tips on how to do that are to set realistic expectations for the results and set timelines for implementation or completion. As the leader you must have conviction in handling disappointments within the organization and you must, as other team members must, accept constructive criticism. It's also important to celebrate achievements and keep all communication channels open.

As a leader, when you respond to a disappointment make sure you manage yourself before confronting the employee or peer. Assume your role in the disappointment if you are part of the cause and assume good intent moving forward. Always focus on the outcome, not the person. Always learn from disappointments to hopefully prevent them from happening again but be prepared if they do.

Many times, you need to motivate after a disappointment. To be able to do that successfully you must first understand what happened. As we have mentioned many times, communication needs to be open. Take the time to discuss and develop a win-win as discussed in handling conflicts and crucial conversations. Provide recognition where warranted and energize the employee and the team by revisiting your vision. Provide appropriate training to the individual if they are disappointed over not attaining a certain position because of lack of skill or knowledge. Most importantly, be supportive of the individual if they are a valued team member.

Performance Planning

Do you remember the old-fashioned performance reviews? Did any of you like them? We doubt it. In fact, even though we've done hundreds of them throughout our careers, we've always hated them. We hated them as employees, and we hated them as managers.

Why is this?

We believe it's because every performance review was a significantly negative event for all. As an employee you usually think that you're better than the review you're being given. As a manager you usually felt like you were knocking the employee down as they felt they were better than your review.

So, let's change the whole context of performance reviews. Let's change them to a meeting that is forward looking and not rearward looking.

Doing performance planning, please review the individual's progress and their contributions to the organization. This is where the KPI's mentioned earlier come into use. If you've set objective KPI's to measure the effectiveness of the team member, they become especially useful now.

There are many ways to put together an evaluation process and document. The key is to establish the expectation for each KPI with a goal and measure the individual's progress to that goal. It can be a numbering system, a lettering system, or whatever works best for you. Measurement can be used to determine raises, bonuses etc.

You need to establish how often a position needs to be reviewed. Quarterly is a good timeframe in today's world, especially with younger workers. Team members should be informed regularly as to their performance.

We have provided an example on the next page.

	Employee Name: _______________	**Title:** _______________

PARAMOUNT
Business Development, Inc.

Evaluation Period: _______________

Supervisor Name: _______________

Rating: 5 - Regularly Exceeds Expectations; 4 - Sometimes Exceeds Expectations; 3 - Meets Expectations; 2 - Sometimes Below Expectations; 1 - Regularly Below Expectations

Company Core Values:

	Score
Value 1: ____	
Value 2: ____	
Value 3: ____	
Value 4: ____	
Value 5: ____	
Value 6: ____	
Value 7: ____	
Value 8: ____	
Average Score	

Personal Goals:

	Score
Goal 1: ____	
Goal 2: ____	
Goal 3: ____	
Goal 4: ____	
Goal 5: ____	
Average Score	

Position Responsibilities

	Score
Attendance and On Time record	
Professionalism - in manner and appearance	
Communicates with Supervisor on daily progress/updates	
Communicates appropriately with Coworkes	
Willing and able to train others	
Takes care of company vehicles and property	
Performs daily tasks in a safe, efficient, high quality method	
Takes care of company tools, machines, and inventory	
Safe driving habits & record	
Keeps work areas clean and organized	
Completes tasks in a timely efficient manner	
Returns company items and inventory to proper location	
Performs tasks according to procedure	
Displays a sense of urgency for time sensitive tasks	
Prioritizes and sets goals appropriately	
Solves problems effectively	
Average Score	

Overall Comments on job performance

Three areas of focus for improvement:

1.

2.

3.

Employee Comments:

Employee Signature _______________   Supervisor's Signature: _______________

Date: _______________   Date: _______________

If a team member is constantly evaluated on the high-performance end of the matrix, there should be some sort of recognition or reward. Recognition and a reward system will make for better retention and will also attract better talent to your organization. Rewards and recognition can come any time, preferably not just at year end.

For rewards and recognitions to be successful, they should be positive, relative, and pertinent to the accomplishment, and they should be timely. People want to be recognized and appreciated. Not all rewards need to be monetary in nature.

This goes back to an earlier chapter of knowing your team members and what motivates them. Some examples are a simple thank you for a job well done, perhaps a team party for a goal accomplishment, a small token gift of appreciation, a plaque or certificate of accomplishment for an increase in grade or something similar, or even recognition in a company publication or email.

On the other end of the spectrum, sometimes team members aren't performing as they should. The best plan is coaching for increased performance. Here is where the "planning" part becomes necessary.

At this point a performance improvement plan (PIP) may be necessary and presented to that individual. While this was discussed earlier as a last step before termination, it could also be useful for an employee who is just not measuring up. Same concept, but different context.

When is a PIP warranted? Criteria to be considered are: can the poor performance be objectively improved by a PIP; do you want the employee to really succeed; was the reason for the poor performance inadequate or poor training; and are there any personal issues affecting performance? If any of these criteria are met, then a PIP may be beneficial.

Individual Development Plans (IDP's)

If you are doing regular performance planning, the next step is easy. Individual Development Plans, or IDP's, are developmental plans for individuals based on the needs for their individual improvement or preparation for future advancement. It allows individual team members to see future opportunities and know what they need to do and learn to attain them. IDP's will keep the team focused and moving in the right direction, maintaining that high-performance culture.

Career Development Plans

Again, moving forward in a logical fashion, the next step is to create career development plans for everyone; these tie tightly to the IDP's and are a logical follow on. Working with your future organizational charts, it should be clear what the future needs are for future positions. You will most likely want to promote from within if possible. A key step in developing the high-potential employees is readying them for those future positions. That planning should start now. For each high-potential employee, you should have their next one – three positions planned out. Each person will need experience, probably training, and probably education for that future position. Plan it out now.

Pay for Performance Plans

Another aspect of high performance is to have an employee pay for performance plan in place for the team. Although team members can be motivated by many things besides money, it will still have an impact regardless of the individual's true motivation. Pay for performance plans can be developed in many ways. The term **"pay for performance"** refers to a reward strategy where an employee will receive higher pay or bonuses for achieving certain performance metrics. This can be in the form of a performance bonus, time off, or merit pay bonus/increase. The metrics can be tied to many things such as goal attainment, sales, gross profit margins, production, etc. The idea is that if the organization performs better, the individuals creating that performance will be rewarded.

Tenure is not a criterion in a pay for performance system. If you pay solely on time of service and not on performance, it is difficult to maintain a high-performing team and culture. Younger employees, whom might be working harder and performing at a higher level will become discouraged by a tenure-based reward system.

Regardless of the pay for performance plan that is put in place it will continue to feed the high-performance culture by keeping team members engaged and focused on the organization's goals.

Emotionally Intelligent Teams & Culture

As you are planning for a high-performance culture, a very important new element is to focus on emotional intelligence. Emotionally intelligent teams have been proven to be more productive, more cohesive, and employee retention is much higher.

There are many facets to an emotionally intelligent culture and this topic is far too expansive to include in this book. However, it is a very important element and should not quickly be dismissed. The younger generations are much more in tune with it and are attracted to it.

Crucial Conversations and Dealing with Conflict

We've talked about having crucial conversations previously in the chapter on clear communication, as well as the importance of resolving conflicts as soon as possible. This is very important to a high-performance culture. If this is not taken care of quickly, the potential harm to the company is escalation in loss of performance. These two items can become a cancer in an organization.

Employee Discipline Plans

Yes, a bad but necessary topic in establishing the rules of the game. Discipline is best dealt with quickly and assertively. An issue with a team member(s) unresolved in a fair and quick manner will have an adverse effect on the rest of the team, even perhaps causing more dissension and lack of focus, ultimately hurting the organization.

Avoidance is a tactic used very often regarding discipline issues. But being fair and quick with the handling of a discipline problem will gain the respect of the team and keep them functioning in their high-performance mode. It will also gain the respect of the individual being disciplined if they truly believe in the culture and are above the line and accountable. It is important to keep discipline in the right context. Effective discipline should not be punitive but meant to encourage the proper behaviors.

Using common sense, gathering all the facts, being an active listener, and offering a just discipline for the issue or behavior is the proper way to handle discipline issues. Further, discipline should be progressive in nature and should be documented. The discipline plan should either be in the employee manual, or in a separate document that is well known.

Termination is always the final step. Before an employee is terminated, there should be thought put into whether this is the right thing to do. Please remember that if the employee has been with you six or more months, you have a lot invested in that person. You have invested training, you have most likely invested employee benefits, and they have probably made friends with the rest of your employees. The point is there is a lot at stake before you just terminate somebody.

Performance Improvement Plan (PIP)

A good last measure is something called a Performance Improvement Plan, or PIP. A PIP is a very deliberate last step plan to save an employee. It's a one to three-page document that identifies the very specific performance issues that need to be corrected. Usually a PIP will list one, to no more than five things that need to immediately be improved. The idea is to put it down on paper and to put a deadline for which definite improvement must be seen.

Developing a PIP is not difficult. Try to keep it as simple as possible. First cite the performance issue(s) objectively. Provide measurable improvement expectations, actions, goals, or metrics that need to be met. There needs to be a time frame established in which the improvement must occur. Be fair but do not extend it longer than is necessary. The best procedure is to put a date on the PIP that is no longer than 90 days into the future. As with delegation, determine the intervals that you will be meeting with the individual or checking on their progress toward improvement. The affected employee should be met with and counseled at the 30- and 60-day point, in the example of a 90-day plan.

Lastly, outline the consequences of not meeting expectations. Determine what those may be from pay reduction to termination. This document must be delivered to and discussed with the affected employee. Ideally the document should be signed by the employee, not as to their agreement, but to their acknowledgement of the document. This document provides the final warning to the affected employee and lets them know in clear and certain terms that their job is on the line. This is an extreme measure, but it does prove effective in certain situations. In the end, if termination ends up being necessary, it is a great document to prove the need for termination if ever questioned.

Last Thought

Do not allow discipline issues to fester. If the issue continues, perhaps they are not a fit for the high-performance culture you have established. As the old saying goes, "one bad apple can spoil the whole bushel." Don't let bad apples spoil your whole bushel. Remember to hire slow and fire fast.

Culture of Learning and Coaching

We have talked about having a strong culture where the rules/parameters are established, and the team has the latitude to operate within those rules to move the organization forward. An important aspect of a good culture is a culture of learning and coaching.

Learning should be encouraged with every leader and team member in the organization. To improve, one must constantly be learning and moving forward. With continual learning and refining, the opportunity to earn more will happen. The learning can be about the industry, the company, or a new skill, it doesn't really matter if everyone continues to learn and encourages others to do the same.

Encouraging learning will not only lead to individual and team success but it will also weave into the culture and rules of the game. Coaching doesn't always have to be a formal process with outside coaches, although it certainly could be beneficial. Having mentors and coaches for key team members and leaders to help them grow and improve can only add value to the organization. And having team members mentor and coach each other formally or informally gives added benefit to them and the organization. Mentoring and coaching will improve the organization because everyone will want to contribute and succeed both individually and collectively.   If there are established rules of the game for the organization and the culture is established and aligned with the vision, it will develop into a high-performance culture.

Chapter 6

Key Number 5: Action Plan

As a business of choice, strong leadership has developed with ever continuing and improving communication among all team members throughout the organization. A solid vision and goals have been established as a destination for the organization and all to follow. And the rules of the game have been established and used to develop a high-energy culture with core values for everyone to live and work by every day. A lot of things are well positioned and in place.

The next critical key component is an action plan, or strategic business plan, for the business. Earlier when we discussed an inspiring vision and core values, we discussed the beginning parts of a solid strategic business action plan.

How does the organization continue to move toward the vision? How does the organization move toward the BOHAG? It is great to know both; it is better to know how to get there from here. The answer is the action plan. People want to know there is a plan to improve, move forward, and achieve goals. Planning is a necessary part of success, yet many organizations and individuals don't do it. <u>Failure to plan is planning to fail.</u>

The 6 P's, Proper Prior Planning Prevents Poor Performance, is what most people should follow. More importantly though, without a plan or roadmap it makes it very hard to get to the destination in a timely manner. Everyone needs to know the plan and the part they play in the execution of the plan. Your job as a top leader is to create this plan.

To create a strategic business action plan, we start with the inspiring vision and BOHAG and break it down into 3-5-year goals. From there we break it into 1-year goals and finally 90-day goals. Sometimes we get questioned why it's 3-5-year goals and not 5-10 or 10-20-year goals. The reason is with as fast paced as today's business world is, 3-5-year goals are all that can successfully be established with any amount of clarity and forethought. Efforts to go further into the future, in our opinion, are a waste of time. The long reaching thoughts are the vision and the BOHAG.

When establishing your goals, 1-year and 90-day goals should be in the **S.M.A.R.T (SEE BELOW)** format. As Stephen Covey says in his book, always begin with the end in mind. That is why we look at the vision and 3-5-year goals and set those as destination points for the organization and then start breaking it down into the smaller chunks of 1-year goals. What needs to be accomplished in the next year to move the organization closer to accomplishing a longer-range goal to move closer to the vision?

Smart Format:
S = specific: meaning that the goal is specific and easy to understand
M = measurable: meaning the goal must lend itself to easy measurement, even if that is only "yes it got done" or "no it did not."
A = achievable: meaning the goals must be reachable in the time frame identified below. For instance, putting a man on Mars is probably not achievable.
R = results oriented: meaning the goal must somehow contribute to the desired results of the organization or contribute to reaching the vision.
T = time oriented: meaning we have due dates.

Establish 1-year goals, preferably no more than 5, in priority order in the **S.M.A.R.T.** format. Once the 1-year goals are established, they need to be broken down into yet even smaller chunks, or 90-day goals. After the 90-day goals are established, strategies need to be picked and executed that will help accomplish those 90-day goals moving you closer to achieving the 1-year goals. The time frame of 90 days is picked because it generally takes several weeks, and perhaps up to 90 days, to determine if the strategies selected are working. If a strategy isn't working within the chosen timeframe, chances are it isn't going to work. Time to change.

The concept of testing and measuring comes into play with the execution of strategies. The effect of the strategy toward goal attainment needs to constantly be assessed. Is it working?   Is it working fast enough? Will it allow achievement of the goal on schedule? if not, pick a new strategy to begin using. Don't stand on principles here. If it is not working, cut it loose and try a different approach!

After picking strategies, the plan is delegation and timing. In simplest terms, "who does what by when". Everyone on the team should have a part in either strategy development or the execution of the strategies. This keeps everyone involved in a part of the planning process and increases buy-in and commitment.

Once the assignments have been made, it is now time for the accountability piece, or the "by when" part of the process. According to the **S.M.A.R.T.** format, goals should be time sensitive, therefore, strategies need to be time sensitive also. Strategies need completion dates which allows everyone on the team to be held accountable in doing their part. This ensures that we continually move the organization forward. Having a solid business plan will keep members involved and attract members that are outcome-focused to the team, and those are the type of members you want to attract.

Again, if you need help in doing your strategic business action plan, read **Fail Safe Planning,** call us, or visit our website.

Chapter 7

Key Number 6: Effective Delegation

Delegation is vitally important to becoming an effective leader. If a leader does not learn how to lead, they will thus become a leader of none. Good delegation attracts individuals to the team and is an important retention tool. Team members recognize that to learn and grow they must accept delegation and know what they are responsible for and to whom they are accountable to. When this happens, everyone is more efficient and effective. It also keeps team members focused and improves communication throughout the organization.

To be able to develop delegation strategies, let's first define delegation. **Delegation** is a **process** wherein the leader or manager assigns responsibility to another member of the team for a project or a task, along with certain authority to accomplish the task.

There are many reasons why people choose not to delegate. And in our opinion, they are all poor excuses. A few common ones are; "it takes too long to explain", "no one else can do it," "if you want it done right, you have to do it yourself", and "the team is overworked and can't take on any more." A leader must overcome excuses to stay above the line and make sure that delegation occurs for improved efficiency and effectiveness. No one can do it all themselves.

What are some good reasons to delegate? It frees up time to do other more critical things; the "important but not urgent" things. It allows business owners to see the big picture and run the business more effectively with more involvement on their part. Delegation also teaches leaders the valuable skill of how to get more done while developing team members' skills. Spreading accountability among team members will build a stronger team with greater trust. A leader can respond more quickly to changes and drive those changes more effectively if there is proper delegation.

A crucial aspect of good delegation is to have an accurate current organizational chart. A leader should also have a future organization chart, about 3-5 years out, based on growth and vision of the company. These, along with good positional agreements, let team members know their responsibilities and accountabilities and provides a chain of command for communication and reporting. An example of a simple organizational chart is shown below.

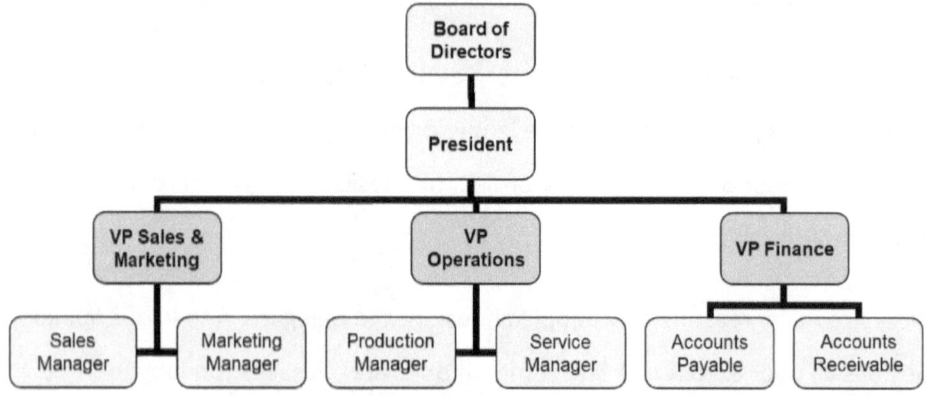

Good leaders and managers leverage their personal time through their people and being able to delegate effectively allows for better leveraging of personnel. As we outline how to effectively delegate, leaders must also guard against abdication.

Delegation without training, authority, and follow up is abdication. When something is delegated with restrictions such as time and/or resources, it is incumbent upon the leader or delegator to check in and make sure appropriate progress is being made, and that the restrictions are not limiting execution of the task. If it is a repeatable task that is learned by the team member, in time, the follow up will be less and less and eventually not needed at all.

There are four key elements of successful delegation: responsibility, authority, training, and accountability.

First, who will be responsible in carrying out the task or event being delegated and why is this the right person? Second, what is the breadth of authority the person being delegated to should have for successful completion of the task or project? Also, things such as spending limits, outside help with achieving the task, etc. The third thing to consider is what training will the person being delegated to need to successfully accomplish the task or project? How can you provide that training? Who should do the training, you or another member of the team? Lastly, how does the delegator hold the person delegated to accountable? Does the task or project need to be completed within a certain time frame or within a certain budget? How often and when will the follow-ups need to occur?

The following is a 7-step process for effective delegation that we prescribe to clients:

1. Choose what needs to be delegated
2. Choose the right person to delegate the task to
3. Communicate what needs to be done to achieve the task, along with a deadline, or completion date
4. Clearly define responsibility and authority
5. Train the person appropriately for successful execution
6. Clarify the results you are expecting, and make sure it is understood
7. Follow up and track step by step

First, a leader must choose what needs to be delegated. Usually it is something that another person could do to take something off the leader's plate, freeing them up to work on other things. As a leader there are two good criteria for picking items to delegate; things you particularly do not enjoy doing, and things you are not particularly good at.

Step 2 is choosing the right person; you must take into consideration their skill level and experience. This is one of the reasons a leader should know as much about their team as possible. Another consideration is the personality of the person chosen. This is important if the task or project involves working with others both inside and outside the organization. Again, as a leader you should know your team members well and know their demeanor, behaviors, and motivators.

Step 3 is to communicate what needs to be done. The communication needs to be clear, concise, and understood. The leader needs to define the task as they perceive it and then communicate the proposed process step by step to get the results that are expected. Ask questions to make sure that what is expected is totally understood by the person chosen for the task. That includes, but not solely restricted to, time frame, budget, manpower, soliciting outside the organization, etc.

Step 4 is to clearly define responsibility and authority. The person who has been delegated the task needs to know the level of responsibility and authority they have been given to complete the task. This ties in to step 3 in that the communication must be clear and concise. If they don't know, there could be a lot of wasted time in having to explain it over again.

Step 5 is often forgotten or skipped over. It is very important to make sure the person being delegated to has the appropriate training to do the task or project. Rarely will an individual already possess all the skills and knowledge necessary. Without the appropriate training given, the delegation will surely fail. Training could come in many shapes and sizes. And it could come from the leader, another employee, or some outside source. For successful delegation, please be sure training is completed.

In step 6 the leader must clarify what is expected upon completion of the project or task. Although the actual outcome may not be known precisely, the expectation of the results needs to be communicated along with a deadline. If at any time during the project the person completing it feels as though there may be a substantial deviation from the expected results, they need to immediately communicate that to the delegator. At that point, the delegator needs to decide to either accept it, or to stop, evaluate, and perhaps start over.

The final step is to follow up and track the task or project step by step. The leader can do this themselves or designate someone else if necessary. Following this delegation process/procedure will provide support to the person doing the task and help ensure successful, timely completion.

Training and developing team members should be a goal of every leader in every organization, and effective delegation is a key part of training and developing team members. Part of delegation is freeing up leaders for bigger responsibilities and growth while delegating to team members expands their knowledge and skills for both short- and long-term growth. It is usually better to develop an internal team member with potential to become more valuable than it is to try and hire that person from the outside. So often leaders and organizations don't invest in training and development of team members and then wonder why team members leave.

Being for Each Other

Effective delegation will get the team working better together once they understand who does what by when. It will create an environment of being for each other and having mutual accountability and support and this is what "teamwork" is all about.

Mutual accountability and support are critical for high-performance teams. You want to foster an environment of teamwork and cooperation. The more you are successful at developing this environment, the more the team will work together synergistically and will become high performing. You want team members pitching in to train each other and help each other when needed.

Honoring Commitments

The more the team understands each other and each other's responsibilities, the more they will hold everyone accountable for individual successes and the success of the organization. Team members will be more willing to support each other and not only win as a team but also lose as a team, maintaining the "above the line" mentality. The key element of accountability is honoring commitments. By honoring commitments, individuals are demonstrating personal accountability and thus holding the team to a higher level. When teams start to perform at a higher level, they continually hold each other accountable to a higher level going forward.

Acknowledgement and Appreciation

Building a culture of mutual support and accountability is an amazing thing. A significant part of effective delegation is acknowledgement of the successful completion of the task or project. Beyond acknowledging the completion, a sincere show of appreciation needs to be given to the person. This is very motivating and inspiring for all to be on a team with these behaviors.

Chapter 8

Key Number 7: 100% Engagement

For a team or organization to be successful you need to have everyone engaged and involved in the progress and movement of the organization. Recent HR surveys over the last 2 years have shown a startling result. Many have reported that the average engagement in the average company is running at about 55%. This is alarming and deplorable. This essentially means that in an 8-hour day, you are getting the equivalent of about 5 hours' worth of productivity. Simply amazing!

Those same studies have shown that in "highly engaged" teams the average engagement is about 85%. This is better, but still seemingly lower than ideal. At 85% that means in an 8-hour day, you are getting the equivalent of 7 hours' worth of productivity. This is a vast improvement over 55%. This is a difference of 2 hours of productivity per employee! That means for every 4 employees you are gaining the productivity of an additional employee.

 If team members don't feel appreciated or motivated, their contributions to the success of the organization will be minimal and they will never feel a part of what you are trying to build. It is especially important now as the workforce is becoming younger that they are engaged and feel as though they are contributing to something larger than themselves. Having everyone engaged and feeling part of the process to goal achievement is also a good retention tool. As we stated earlier, the whole premise of this book is to create an environment that people want to become a part of and remain with to finish their careers.

Team Alignment

One of the first things that is critical to higher engagement is getting a high level of team alignment. As a leader, you need to have everyone on the team aligned around the vision, BOHAG, core values, core purpose, core why, and goals. A team alignment meeting is a communication and planning session that gets everyone on the same page. It reviews vision, BOHAG, core values, core purpose, core why, goals, expectations of the team, and who does what by when. This is so everyone knows their part in the success of the organization, be it individually or departmentally. This meeting will create buy-in and inclusion. This is very important going forward to keep everyone engaged and keeping their eye on the prize.

Setting the Tone

During the team alignment activities, it is important for the leader to "set the tone." For example, when discussing the vision, values, and BOHAG, the leader must show his/her passion for the business and the future. The team needs to feel the leader's passion and see the leader walking the talk. True passion is infectious and is very important to a highly engaged team. Authentic behaviors are also very important. Inauthenticity will be picked up in a nano second and will completely turn off and demotivate the team.

Getting Higher Engagement

There are some aspects of 100% engagement that are fundamental; one of those is having everyone know their role and responsibility within the organization and the importance of their role because it will improve collaboration within your organization. Another aspect is having a culture of support in which people know who and where to go to for help. This leads to stronger teams and will improve overall effectiveness and efficiencies within the organization. It also makes movement within the organization, such as handovers or transitions, happen easier.

Engaging All Generations

We think today that engaging all generations is a new thing. We, as the current older generation, lament the days of old and the younger generations. Hogwash.

Here is the secret: Our grandparents and parents felt the same way about us!

Discussing the differences in generations and how to deal with these differences is well outside the context and purpose of this book. However, fortunately for you, there are many current resources you can tap into to learn about the generational differences. Just be sure you are utilizing a credible resource.

Effectively engaging all generations will create a high-performance culture. Many companies have figured this out. Good examples are Google, Apple, Enterprise Rent-A-Car, Southwest Airlines, and many others. You can do this too!

Once you understand the generational differences, you as the leader must set the tone for intergenerational communication and cooperation. You need to provide the tools and insist that all team members work seamlessly together despite differences in gender, religion, and age i.e. generational differences. Again, it is up to you to set the tone, especially on these matters!

Creating Momentum & Cohesiveness

Communication should be given high consideration in increasing team engagement. While most people do not like meetings, they can be an efficient method of communicating and keeping everyone on the same page. However, we are not believers of having meetings for the sake of having meetings. How you run team meetings is an important part of increasing engagement.

First, have a clear purpose for the meeting and consider holding it at consistent intervals. A key is to make sure the content is well prepared and there is a plan for the meeting with preparation requirements for those attending the meeting. Always have an agenda for the meeting and send it out prior to the meeting if possible so attendees can prepare.   Meetings are best used for communication, analysis, debate, and decision making.

Be sure you start and end on time or you will lose credibility. It is important to stay on topic and track; avoid excess discussion or going down rabbit holes and adjust topics as strategically needed. Small changes in the agenda keep the meeting fresh. As the leader of the meeting, it is your job to encourage participation and get everyone involved.

Be aware of overcontrolling the meeting and disregarding other's statements and contributions. Your goal should be to get 100% involvement. Encourage this, as necessary. A good idea for inclusion and involvement would be to designate a different person every meeting to take notes. Afterwards, distribute the notes with the recap, action items, and assignments.

Running effective meetings has many benefits such as keeping everyone in the loop and allowing interaction with each other which enhances team performance. If done well it gets keeps them prepared and continually participating.

Effective meetings can energize the team and raise morale which makes for better teamwork. Improved teamwork leads to increased productivity and potentially increased profitability. Meetings can continue to move things forward which is important to keep team members engaged, retain good people, and attract good people.

The final point in this section about improving momentum and cohesiveness is to engage the whole team in the planning process for the company. Sometimes this may be difficult to do, but it is important for the team to know that they have input in the direction of the organization and that their contribution helps the overall success of the organization. If they contribute in helping to set the course for the organization, team members will take ownership of the direction and seek to make it as successful as it can be.

Building Your Team for the Future

As you work to become the employer of choice you need to consider building your team for the future needs of the company and to simultaneously be doing succession planning. The one constant is that things change. That is why you establish a vision to consistently be moving forward and preparing for the changes that will come as best you can. Hence designing future organizational charts.

Looking to develop future leaders and having career paths within the organization will retain your good employees and attract others who want to be part of your team. Training will prepare them for their future roles and lets others know you are a progressive organization and a good place to work. This will be a magnet, especially to the younger generations.

Succession planning is something that should be done from the day you open the company. None of us will live forever and we all must be replaced at some point. (For more on succession planning, read our book "Succession Planning for the Rest of Us," available on Amazon.)

Ongoing succession planning is key for grooming future leaders within your organization. If your future leaders are involved in the process, they will see the possibilities that are in front of them and what they can aspire to. They will also continuously perform at levels which will benefit the team and the organization. Succession planning also helps retain, motivate, and engage future leaders in the success of the organization.

Succession planning for the team of your future should include the vital elements mentioned previously such as IDP's, career planning, and performance planning. Using all these tools synergistically as part of succession planning will greatly increase your success.

Putting It All Together

To become the employer of choice you need to become the leader and develop the team and culture that will attract people to you.

As a leader you need to continually communicate to move things forward in the organization and toward achievement of goals. Some items that consistently need to be communicated are the vision, values, BOHAG, and goals of the company. Your job is to keep everyone focused.

It is also important to communicate the present status of the company, the progress achieved on attaining the goals of the company, and openly discuss any setbacks that are preventing movement forward. By communicating these updates, it eliminates negativity and unsubstantiated rumors. No communication is not acceptable.

As the future workforce changes, every step in building your team is important in attracting and retaining the right people to continue to grow your organization. Follow the steps we presented, and you will build an organization that you will be proud of and people will want to join.

If you need help or have questions; contact us at:

Paramount Business Development

570-517-7100

www.paramountbusinessdevelopment.com

Don't forget about our other books available on Amazon.

Sales Magic – 12 Steps to Achieving Massive Sales Growth

Fail Safe Planning

Succession Planning for the Rest of US